A ROOKIE READER

PAUL THE PITCHER

Written and Illustrated
By Paul Sharp

Prepared under the direction of Robert Hillerich, Ph.D.

CHILDRENS PRESS®

CHICAGO

This book is for Seth

Library of Congress Cataloging in Publication Data

Sharp, Paul.
  Paul the pitcher.

  (A Rookie reader)
  Summary: Rhymed text describes the different things
  Paul enjoys when he throws a ball. Includes word list.
  [1. Baseball—Fiction.   2. Stories in rhyme]
  I. Title. II. Series.
  PZ8.3.S532Pau 1984   [E]   84-7071
  ISBN 0-516-02064-1

Paul the pitcher throws a ball.

Baseball is the game for Paul.

Paul the pitcher throws a ball.

He throws the ball
from spring till fall.

9

He throws it to the catcher's mitt,

unless the batter gets a hit.

Paul the pitcher loves to throw,

sometimes high,

sometimes low.

Paul the pitcher loves to throw,

sometimes fast,

sometimes slow.

To throw the ball is lots of fun,

unless the batter gets a run.

Paul the pitcher loves to throw.

Someday he'd like to be a pro.

WORD LIST

	gets	Paul
a	he	pitcher
ball	he'd	pro
baseball	high	run
batter	hit	slow
be	is	someday
catcher's	it	sometimes
fall	like	spring
fast	lots	the
for	loves	throw(s)
from	low	till
fun	mitt	to
game	of	unless

About the Author/Illustrator

Paul Sharp graduated from the Art Institute of Pittsburgh with a degree in Visual Communications.

He has done illustrations for numerous children's books and magazines. This is the fifth book Paul has illustrated for Childrens Press. He also wrote it.

Paul presently lives, and works as an artist, in Lafayette, Indiana.